"In *Be (Extra)Ordinary*, Maryanne's passion is matched only by her empathy for her fellows. She is the proverbial best friend you haven't met yet. And so much more than a survivor, she is what I call a thriver. I have always found her writing a joy to read, fluid and infectious!"

—SCOTT SCHIAFFO, Actor, musician, and author

"Maryanne Christiano-Mistretta reveals in detail her unresentful journey through her trials as a child of divorced parents, a target of bullies, and her growth into a strong, self-respecting, confident woman who loves herself (as we all should). I recommend this book as a must read for all parents who are about to send a child, girl or boy, off to school and out from under the protection of the home nest."

—OLEDA BAKER, Model, author, and entrepreneur

"(This book) forced me to take a deeper look into my own insecurities and how to combat the feelings of not fitting in. ... If we could all be as honest about ourselves as the author, we would have a better understanding of how to navigate the choppy waters of life."

—ROBYN LANE, Music director, WRAT radio, New Jersey

Be (EXTRA)ORDINARY

TEN WAYS TO BECOME YOUR OWN *Hero*

MARYANNE CHRISTIANO-MISTRETTA

KiCam
PROJECTS

LIBRARY OF CONGRESS CATALOGING-IN-PUBLICATION DATA
Names: Christiano-Mistretta, Maryanne, author.
Title: Be (extra)ordinary : ten ways to become your own hero / by
Maryanne
Christiano-Mistretta.
Description: Georgetown, Ohio : KiCam Projects, [2019].
Identifiers: LCCN 2019017993 (print) | LCCN 2019020979 (ebook)
| ISBN
9781733546232 (ebook) | ISBN 9781733546225
Subjects: LCSH: Self-actualization (Psychology) | Happiness.
Classification: LCC BF637.S4 (ebook) | LCC BF637.S4 C499687
2019 (print) |
DDC 158.1--dc23
LC record available at https://lccn.loc.gov/2019017993

Cover and book design by Mark Sullivan

ISBN 978-1-7335462-2-5 (paperback)
ISBN 978-1-7335462-3-2 (e-book)

Printed in the United States of America

Published by KiCam Projects
Georgetown, Ohio

www.KiCamProjects.com

Dedicated to our dear kitty, Bennie Cat
(Bennie Grover Hemingway) in Heaven.

Dearest Bennie,

You were only in our lives a very short time. We rescued you as a young feral. You trusted us. You let us pet you. You were more interested in love than in our free food. I'd never seen another cat lift his head to be petted while he was eating. You were the cutest and my all-time favorite cat. The vet checked you out and told us you had FIV and, therefore, possibly a short life. Little did we know how short. You were only three years old. Five months after we took you in, we learned you had a brain tumor on that precious, pretty little head of yours. You little fighter, you gave it your best shot. Your determination to live in spite of your unfortunate circumstances is a big lesson for anyone going through a tough time. You're forever loved in our hearts, and you will never be forgotten. You are my hero!

table of contents

What does the word "hero" mean to you?

Who do you view as a hero? It could be a celebrity or a friend or family member. Maybe you admire first responders, military members, or veterans.

Everyone defines "hero" differently. Personally, I truly believe we all have a hero inside us. That's why I wrote this book: to inspire everyone to live life to the fullest and be the best they can be.

To do that, it's important to surround yourself with people who support your dreams, make you smile, and give you a reason to want to be with them. This is the world I've created for myself—a world of heroes.

As you read my book and see snippets of my life, you'll learn about people I view as heroes. I hope this motivates you to think about your own heroes, as well as how you've been a hero to others. You probably are already a hero in many ways. I'd like to multiply that by ten so that after you finish this book, you'll feel like a superhero!

It's not difficult to be a hero. Sometimes it can mean doing something grand, but much of the time it's about simple things, such as offering a smile to a passing stranger in a grocery store. You never know who needs you and who will be touched by you just because you're being your super-cool self. As I like to say, "Be YOUnique!"

We're all capable of doing great things, and everything we do—big or small—makes a difference. In this book, you'll learn that I've taken cues from so many different kinds of people over the years. Whether it was a beloved person in my life, a rock star, a mentor, a best friend, or a homeless person, each in his or her own way showed me what a hero looks like and how to be one.

From my experiences, I vulnerably share with you my tips and tools for becoming your own hero.

Are you ready?

One…two…three…Become your own hero!

chapter one

(BE)DEDICATED TO YOURSELF

"Just be yourself" is something we're taught early on. Seems easy enough, right? Then why is it that when we're completely ourselves, it often feels awkward?

Learning to be yourself is something you should have nailed by your early twenties. But peer pressure can rear its ugly head well into adulthood.

Think about yourself today. How often do you find yourself saying yes to things you don't want to do just because your friends are doing them? Do you hear yourself saying yes to things that aren't really *you*?

For instance, would you put "a trip to Hawaii" or "owning a Lamborghini" on your bucket list? Is that truly *your* dream? Or is it what your friends dream about?

Do you go to events where you know you'll be bored, but you attend anyway to make others happy?

Saying no to people you care about is hard because you don't want to hurt anyone's feelings. Think back to when you were a child. Your mother wanted you to clean your room, but you wanted to play. "Do it for me," she'd say. And so you would.

So, it's in our subconscious to do things we don't want to do because we are doing them for someone else. In the meantime, though, what are we doing for ourselves?

Not being true to yourself leads to dissatisfaction with life. If you always do things for other people and not yourself, before you know it, you start harboring resentment. The more you give to please others, the worse it can be for you—and possibly for your loved ones too.

But once you begin putting yourself first, you become happier and, therefore, more willing to give to others!

Here's how to start: Each day, set small goals for yourself. Whether it's building your confidence or pushing yourself to do something that's good for your career, get at least one thing done. At the end of the day, it's important to write down your accomplishments, including the date. This way, when you look back a year later, you'll see how far you've come. How cool will it be when you realize that some of the things you wished to achieve actually manifested?

Perhaps there are some things that haven't happened—yet. Or, maybe while other triumphs were transpiring, you changed your priorities. You now realize some of the things you used to want are no longer necessary in your life. That's part of growth—being flexible as you learn more about yourself.

Once you've reached some of your own goals and built up your self-confidence, you can start helping other people achieve their dreams.

When I was a journalist, it was exciting to write for the entertainment section of the newspaper and interview aspiring young musicians. Their enthusiastic voices spoke passionately about their dreams.

Does the name Nick Jonas sound familiar to you? I interviewed him for *The Montclair (New Jersey) Times* years before the Jonas Brothers were a household name.

Nick Jonas came into my office with his mom. He was delighted to be interviewed for a newspaper, and he was polite, well-spoken, and charming. He began acting in theater at the age of seven and released his debut album in 2004 at the age of twelve, a year or so after I interviewed him.

It was always a thrill to help give young hopefuls a start with publicity, and that never could have happened if I hadn't had conviction in my writing and interviewing skills. That's how it works: You become sure of yourself, and then you elevate others.

When I was growing up, one of my greatest inspirations was Freddie Mercury of Queen. His essence vibrated with confidence; he lived life to the fullest. During the time I was buying the early Queen albums, I was relentlessly bullied in school. But I'd come home, close the door to my bedroom, and play all the albums after I did my homework. The music took me to another place—a place where I was self-assured and happy. I'd stay up late on the weekends to watch Queen on television shows such as "Don Kirshner's Rock Concert" and "The Midnight Special." I'd copy Freddie Mercury's stage moves and practice them in the mirror. I'd go to school with my fingernails painted black on only my left hand, just like Freddie.

Though we all should be encouraged to be ourselves, a great starting point is to emulate someone you admire until you can "make it your own." Modeling myself after Freddie Mercury in my youth enabled me to develop confidence when I was lacking it. I read every book about Queen that I could get my hands on. I added "dear" and "darling" to my sentences like Freddie did. Relating to Freddie Mercury and his music gave me a safety net. The music of Queen was like having a friend I could depend on.

That's why when Queen reunited, first with Paul Rodgers in 2005 and then later with Adam Lambert, it never bothered me that another singer was filling in for the late Freddie. Carrying on Freddie's legacy was a genius idea, and both Rodgers and Lambert did an amazing job.

Lambert, in particular, stole my heart because he was so humble. He bowed to Brian May and shared with Queen fans that he, too, was a fan and was not there to replace Freddie.

In my research on Lambert, I came across a website called BullyVille, where Lambert shared that he had been a victim, bullied by small-minded people because of his sexuality. Freddie Mercury also had been bullied, for his overbite.

Both men stayed true to themselves, overcame their obstacles, and went on to become great successes. Bullies tend to pick on people they are jealous of. They see something unique or special in their victims—something they feel they lack. They don't know how to cope, so they lash out.

While the victim is confident enough to embrace his or her uniqueness, he or she also must develop the confidence to stand up and take on bullies when necessary. Trying to keep your confidence up while finding out who you are *and* developing your skills and style *and* being bullied is no easy feat! It's a daily work in progress. A major "trick" to help along the way is simply taking care of yourself. (Do you see a pattern here? It always goes back to you helping YOU!)

So, make time to get in the gym or practice an exercise routine at home. Drink alcohol in moderation (if at all) and choose homemade meals ninety percent of the time. Save restaurants for weekends or celebrations— don't make them a way of life. Your body will thank you.

Stay conscious of who you are and what you want. Keep positive messages in view. There's nothing wrong with having the words "You are beautiful" taped to your bathroom mirror or using your computer screensaver to remind you of your financial goal for the year. Don't be oblivious to these messages. Read them every day and embed them in your brain until they become part of you.

Some people like to create dream boards. A dream board, also known as a vision board, is a collage of images and affirmations of your dreams and desires. It's a great source of inspiration and motivation to help you manifest your professional and personal goals.

And don't keep your dream-board visions to yourself. When you share with good friends and family, they can help you reach your goals, and they'll be there to revel with you when you succeed.

I remember creating my first dream board. A month went by...nothing. Two months went by...nothing. Three months went by...still nothing. I was beginning to lose my momentum in creatively visualizing my future. So, after a few weeks of frustration, I redirected my mind-set and changed my irritation to celebration. I stopped allowing myself to be disenchanted and started taking the steps to get where I wanted to go.

For example, there was one thing I was doing in my career that was lucrative, but it was not serving me in the long run. I'd been offering a program for libraries for three years, but it had started to feel like a chore. So, even though the money was great, I decided to let the program go. I was done with it. I took the program off my website and stopped booking it. Once I stopped doing something that wasn't making me happy, I had more time to invest in myself. With this extra time, I joined a group to help me become a better speaker.

After I took action, by the fourth month of my vision

board, I started to see things manifesting. My dream board was becoming a *reality* board.

Here's my challenge to you: Look closely at your career or how you are filling your time. If you're doing something and it's not making you happy—even though you are making money—you might want to question whether that path is still for you. It's a big leap of faith, but taking time off or making a change is a great investment in pursuing something that will make you much happier. You might have to tighten the budget for a bit, so of course, make a plan before you make a move. But do note that time is its own currency. The more time you spend unhappy, the more time you lose.

Making your dreams reality is not easy. It takes much more than just believing. It takes action—and also a little luck. If your dreams don't come true right away, don't take that personally. If you're not picked for the team, the job, or the promotion, it doesn't mean you failed. Maybe it just wasn't your time or it wasn't meant to be. Sometimes we can look back on our lives and see that not getting the one thing we just *knew* we needed was the best thing that could have happened to us. Your time will come, so don't give up. Keep pushing forward. Next time around, you'll be the chosen one. Or, you might wind up going in a whole new direction. Life is great that way.

Case in point: Between working in a corporate office and becoming a full-time professional writer, I used to be a waitress at a coffee shop. It was hard being a wait-ress, and I just wasn't a good one. Criticized by the seasoned waitresses who worked there, as well as the coffee shop owners, I lost my self-esteem. That job did a number on me!

I stayed there longer than I should have because the coffee shop was in an artsy town and I connected with cool people who were patrons. Friends who lived in the area would come visit me too. Plus, since I was single and living alone, I appreciated getting at least two free meals there per day. But it was obvious I didn't belong there. Right after my shift, I either hung out with friends or went home to write. Sometimes I'd be up writing poetry or articles until the wee hours of the morning. I was a classic writer's cliché: I'd return to work the next day with red, tired eyes. At my lowest point, I'd take a shot of tequila before I hopped on the bus to go to work. The job was consuming my inner being. A year later, the movie *Heavy* came out. I related to Liv Tyler's character, Callie, a soft-spoken college drop-out who had a sad life working as a waitress.

Finally, I complained to a friend how much I hated the job.

That friend said something genius that ended up changing my life: "Would you rather be a good waitress or a good writer?"

There certainly is nothing wrong with being a good waitress (or waiter). But my friend's insight made me realize there was a bigger world out there for *me*, and I needed to fully pursue that. Shortly after I had that discussion with him, I quit the waitress job and ended up working full time at my first magazine.

Here's how it happened: I answered a newspaper ad. When I met with the publisher, he liked me right away because of my enthusiasm. "I've never met someone as excited as you are to work here," he told me. At that first meeting, I made the mistake of telling him I was also working as a waitress, which made him hesitant to hire me. He didn't want me to quit my waitress job—my only reliable source of income—in case the magazine job didn't work out.

So, in the beginning, I worked for the magazine part time, doing various tasks in the evening. I'd work my waitress shift, catch the 3 p.m. train to Hoboken, New Jersey, and sometimes work as late as eleven at the magazine.

In the meantime, I continued to be frustrated with my waitress job until I finally got the nerve to give my notice. It was irrational to leave for a part-time position, but I knew I didn't belong there anymore—I never really had. My time was up, and I had higher aspirations.

When I told the publisher I'd quit my waitressing job, he immediately hired me full time as his assistant. Then, I worked my way around the company until I befriended the editor, who took me under her wing. Next thing I knew, my first feature article was published worldwide!

It all happened because I trusted what I knew about my true self—my skills, my passions, my dreams—and I started taking the steps to make my vision become a reality.

Being dedicated to yourself is hard work. The thing is, once your mentality shifts and you start being true to who you really are, you gain confidence and good things happen. It might seem like magic, but it's not. The key is to be consistent. And most of all, be *YOUnique*!

chapter two

(BE)VULNERABLE

Not too long ago, I experienced one of the most incredible things in my life. I attended Lewis Howes's "Summit of Greatness" in Columbus, Ohio. It was a two-day seminar featuring one great motivational speaker after another.

Mind you, I'd never heard of any of them, but one of my best girlfriends wanted me to accompany her on a ten-hour road trip. Motivational speakers were not on my radar. I assumed this journey would end in some sort of New Agey yoga retreat.

Then I was blown away by two full days of nothing but inspiration and positivity—magnified to the fullest! When I returned home, I was pumped for several weeks. High on life. High on my dreams. High on the possibilities.

What struck me most was Howes's speech on being vulnerable. He shared a horrific story about being raped at the age of five by the teenaged son of his babysitter. (You can hear Howes speak about his story in his podcast "What Sharing My Childhood Rape Taught Me About Being a Loving, Vulnerable, Free Man.") He explains why he carried the weight for so long and the lessons he learned along the way. One of the lessons he shares is that holding on to resentment is not serving you. "It's holding you back from your greatness," he says in his podcast.

What does it mean to be vulnerable? First, you have to accept the fact of what is happening or has happened. Then you can express your concern to a trusted friend or partner. Sharing your feelings and talking about your pain are what being vulnerable is all about. Attacking someone with words or actions to retaliate gives you a false sense of security. You need to elevate yourself to a point where someone else's opinion of you is just that— merely an opinion. Your sense of self-worth should depend on one thing and one thing only: what *you* think of yourself!

Being vulnerable means believing you are worthy, that you have the right to feel your emotions and to tell your story. You have the right to be heard.

The coolest thing about being vulnerable is the truth of it. It means you do not downplay a situation to make yourself look better. Honesty and vulnerability are so liberating. With both, you just be who you are. Then the real magic comes when you see who truly sticks with you, as well as the new people who come into your life.

The hard part about being vulnerable is that you can share a part of your true self and be rejected for it. Or, maybe even worse, you might be met with indifference.

If that's the case, then those people are not your people—even if they're family. One of my favorite mantras is "Go where the love is."

Being vulnerable also means being strong. You put yourself out there and risk rejection. Sometimes it might hurt, but most of the time, it will be well worth it.

Take Lewis Howes, for example. He is just one of many men—including Terry Crews, Michael Gaston, and Alex Winter—who have spoken out about their experiences with sexual harassment and assault, joining the Me Too movement initially begun by women. High-profile actresses such as Rose McGowan, Gwyneth Paltrow, Ashley Judd, Jennifer Lawrence, and Uma Thurman were incredibly brave to speak out about being terrified and humiliated, not knowing how people would react.

The Me Too movement began in 2006 on the now-ancient social network Myspace. It was part of a campaign to promote "empowerment through empathy." Knowing there is strength in numbers and speaking out about being a survivor can take a big weight off your shoulders and allow you to move on to excellence.

Anti-bullying movements also have embraced vulnerability, and that has resonated with me in particular. It took me a very long time to become vulnerable regarding my experiences being bullied in grade school and high school. I didn't realize how much the shame of it was holding me back. I never talked about it. Perhaps deep down, I believed some of the things the bullies said to me, that I was ugly, a scumbag, and a dog (they barked at me when I passed them in the hallways). I was told I was dumb and spacey and mocked for my Italian heritage. Children made fun of my clothes and my eyeglasses.

I was no stranger to feeling bad about myself. I came from a single-mom household. I never knew why I didn't have a father, but I assumed it was my fault. I must have done something wrong. When I grew older and saw close relationships other girls had with their fathers, I thought there must have been something terribly not right about me. *Why is she so loved and I'm not?*

I wanted to disappear. So, I simply stopped talking. But that only made me stand out more, which intensified the bullying.

Looking back, I don't know why I carried the shame with me for so long. Bullying is barbaric and sadistic. Bullies are the real embarrassment; the victims have nothing to be embarrassed about. Bullies should feel ashamed. Confident people don't bully others. Happy people don't bully others.

I'll never forget the year I realized the shameful burden I was carrying with me, two whole decades after my high school bullying ended. I subconsciously allowed myself to be bullied by adults! It was summertime and I was out of work. While unemployed and working sparingly as a freelancer, I was hanging out with a bunch of bohemians—writers, musicians, and artists, also out of work, barely getting by on their art. Their ages ranged from twenties to forties, and it didn't take me long to realize that for them to feel important, they thrived on trashing others either directly, via gossip, or over the Internet. Eventually, they included me, taking cheap shots and writing falsehoods about me online. It was adult bullying at its finest—or, I should say, at its worst.

As a person who always took pride in working, always doing overtime, and never calling in sick, I felt like such a loser for not working that summer. It's no wonder I lacked confidence and therefore attracted other people who weren't happy with themselves and took it out on others. Within two months, it was obvious these people were not my people, so I stopped hanging out with them. Once I dropped the negativity from my life, within a month I landed yet another dream job in journalism. Positive actions get positive results!

Still, I continued to carry the shame of being bullied. I never put two and two together that it was not my fault. Throughout my adulthood, I blamed myself for every person who didn't like me. Then I allowed several untruths to sink deep into my psyche: I thought that once I became successful, people would like me because success meant I was smart, and I thought once I was married, people would like me because marriage meant I was lovable. And the biggest untruth of all was that if I was nice to everybody, everybody would like me. With that, I developed a terrible habit: I became a people pleaser.

The truth is, not everyone is going to like you, no matter what. Think of someone famous whom you admire, then look up their name on YouTube. Out of thousands of "thumbs up" reactions, you will see at least several hundred "thumbs down." That is proof that no matter how great someone is, someone else is going to have something negative to say.

Here's an example. I thought of someone the world embraced, someone who was known for all her good deeds. I went to YouTube and put in "The People's Princess" and found a short documentary on the life of Princess Diana. Thousands of people gave the video a thumbs up. And of course, a couple hundred people gave it the thumbs down.

Now, if a couple hundred people don't like Princess Diana, that should take some of the pressure off you, right?

Once I was able to accept the truth that not everyone is going to like me no matter how hard I try, I could just be myself, and my social life got better. I not only have a very happy marriage, I have amazing girlfriends. I can be honest with everyone in my life. I have no shame about saying, "I was bullied," because it's the truth. And it wasn't my fault.

Howes's experiences were terrible. When he became vulnerable enough to share them, he freed himself from their power. For me, when I started sharing about my experiences being bullied, a weight was lifted. I felt so free and so relieved. From that moment on, all the bullies no longer had an impact on my psyche.

I remember the first time I publicly admitted I was bullied. I was writing an article for a newspaper about a debate at a local school. One team was saying it was important to address the issue of bullying, whereas the other team was saying there were more important things to tackle in school.

Of course, as a journalist, I wasn't allowed to be biased. But after the debate, I felt a strong urge to address one of the young girls who said she was bullied. She was so beautiful but seemed so fragile. Her eyes were huge, with a deep sadness behind them. I wanted to give her a big hug; my heart just went out to her. Instead, I stayed professional.

I encouraged her to stay strong, then added, "Do you know who else was bullied?"

"Who?" she asked shyly.

"Me," I said. After a pause, I added, "And it turned out okay."

She smiled softly.

I left hoping I had given her a glimmer of optimism. And truth be told, I gave myself a dose of optimism too. I felt a huge sense of relief. That little girl might never know how much she did for me. If my words helped her, she certainly helped me even more. By being vulnerable, I was able to make peace with troubling memories of my youth. Confronting my past was much better than hiding from it. Now moving forward, I felt I could freely empathize with others who struggled the way I did, because I was no longer a victim of shame.

Embracing my vulnerability helps me build stronger bonds with people. It seems that whenever I share that I was bullied, there's a woman—or man—who says, "Me too!"

When I give speeches on being bullied, I meet people who also were bullied who have grown to be extremely successful in their lives, making six- or seven-figure salaries. They did not let their experiences of being bullied stop them! And they have no qualms about saying, "I was bullied too." They are brave to be vulnerable, and they are not living with shame.

I keep adding people to my "tribe" who are honest, vulnerable, and successful regardless of what they went through in life. By being vulnerable, more doors have opened for me, in both business and friendships.

Vulnerability can help you weed out negative people in your life. There's a popular Internet meme that says, "Some people are going to reject you simply because you shine too bright for them. And that's okay. Keep shining."

Let those people reject you and move on. You're too good for them. Smart, kind, confident, successful people rarely treat others poorly. They don't need to belittle people to feel better about themselves, because they like who they are. These are the types of people with whom you want to share your vulnerability. And that will make them comfortable to share their vulnerability with you.

When two people are vulnerable with each other, that's truly an honest friendship. It's so liberating to be able to share authentic feelings. What comes after sharing something scary is a higher level of confidence. That is the gift you get for being courageous and staying true to yourself.

Once you get to that point, it won't bother you when others don't like you. Because now, you have these great friends you can share bad stuff with—and they still love you. They've seen your weak spots. They've seen what makes you sad. And they see you when you're not at your best. But guess what: It's okay!

By letting your guard down, you are risking having people take advantage of your feelings and hurting you. But being too proud to let your guard down and always presenting yourself as perfect means you are leading with your ego, pretending to be something you're not. People can see when you're being fake or hiding something. When people lie, or lead with their ego, it means they haven't learned the beauty of vulnerability yet.

There's nothing wrong with showing others you are human. You make mistakes. You face struggles and sadness. You have feelings. You've been hurt. That's life.

Embracing vulnerability will give you the strength, and the support, you need to get through the bad times and be the glorious, successful person you were born to be.

chapter three

(BE)UNIQUE

As you've seen, I like to personalize the word "unique" by spelling it YOUnique, because it truly is about being *you*.

As children, we have very little say about things in our life. Our parents dress us, feed us, and provide entertainment for us. Then as we grow, we develop our own likes and styles. At first, it's usually telling our parents what toys we want. Then it moves into what we want to wear and then into what we want to do. Many children are inspired by what other children are doing. But there are those who find their inspiration elsewhere—those who don't follow the crowd.

Last Christmas, I read a disturbing comment on social media by a woman who'd watched the classic *Rudolph the Red-Nosed Reindeer* for the first time. She wrote that she'd feel uncomfortable watching the movie with her grandchildren because of all the bullying.

The woman had missed the point completely.

Rudolph is practically the patron saint of uniqueness. He was picked on because of his inimitable red nose, which made him stand out. His nose was considered an embarrassment by the other reindeer. But that very same nose, the one thing that made him different, is what made him a hero. On a foggy Christmas Eve, Rudolph's shiny nose led the way for Santa's sleigh!

In the previous chapter, I mentioned the Summit of Greatness. Another speaker there was Amy Purdy, an actress, model, para-snowboarder, motivational speaker, clothing designer, and author.

At the age of nineteen, Purdy contracted a form of bacterial meningitis that affected her circulatory system when the infection led to septic shock. She lost both kidneys, her spleen had to be removed, and both of her legs were amputated below the knee.

Incredibly, Purdy began snowboarding just seven months after receiving her prosthetic legs and eventually participated in several snowboarding competitions. She was even on "Dancing with the Stars."

When I saw Purdy speak, tears ran down my face. I thought to myself, *This woman did more in her life with no legs than most people do with two!* For the next month, every time I thought about complaining—about anything—I stopped myself because of Amy Purdy. *You have your health; you have both legs; you have nothing to complain about.*

Instead of letting a tragedy stand in her way, Purdy used it to her advantage. When I saw her on stage, her prosthetic legs looked so real, she even had feet with painted toes. Adorable! And truly unique.

Lizzie Velasquez, author of *Dare to be Kind*, was born with Marfanoid-progeroid-lipodystrophy syndrome, an extremely rare congenital disease that prevents her from accumulating body fat and gaining weight. She's never weighed more than sixty-four pounds, even consuming between five thousand and eight thousand calories per day. Since being dubbed "World's Ugliest Woman" in a video someone posted on YouTube in 2006 when Lizzie was seventeen, she has spoken out against bullying. Her YouTube videos have received more than fifty-four million views.

The thing is, Lizzie is not ugly at all. She has amazing hair, she's stylish, and in each photo of her, she is smiling. Different? Yes! Ugly? No way! And if you read Lizzie's book or watch her TED Talk, you'll see she has the heart of an angel. She's funny too.

These are examples of heroes who have elevated themselves because life dealt them cards that made them incredibly different. There are also myriad individuals who were born no different, physically, than anyone else but who have become standouts because of their uniqueness.

Whether your uniqueness is something you were born with or something you've developed because it is in your heart, it can come with both a price and a reward.

My friend George is the most confident guy I know. From the time we were teenagers, he knew he was good-looking and that he was a great guy, too. (He's always had something nice to say about others.) Before "big hair" was a big deal in the 1980s, George was one of the first to start doing it. I asked him if people made fun of him for his hair.

He said, "Yes, all the time. But then there will always be that one cool guy who approaches you and says, 'Dude, you have great hair!'"

So, to George, being different was worth it.

Because I was bullied for dressing differently from other kids in high school, when I reached twenty, I went in the opposite direction and dressed conservatively for a few years. But guess what: It didn't make a difference; my soul still marched to the beat of a different drummer. I read more books than the average person. I wasn't into petty gossip. I preferred my own company to being in a group. If people bad-mouthed someone, I wouldn't participate. Whether I liked it or not, I still stood out.

Then around the time of the grunge rock era, I started to dress more like my true self, the person I was back then. I embraced the T-shirts, the jeans, the black boots, and the flannel shirts. I got my first tattoo. I let my hair grow very long. I even pierced my nose. People constantly were on my case about it, saying it was "ugly" and asking, "Did that hurt?" Someone even said I looked like a bull and he wanted to pull me by my nose ring.

But still, I loved my nose ring. I ignored the negative comments and just went on with my life until I got bored with the ring and took it out.

To this day, I tend to stand out a bit. I go back and forth between dying my hair crimson red or plum-crazy purple. I wear dark eyeliner every day. And I'm a huge fan of Katy Perry's whimsical shoe line. I have at least fifteen boxes of her awesome shoes!

It's not that I *try* to be different. I don't follow styles; I just like what I like. I present myself the way I feel comfortable. I'm not flamboyant or outrageous by any means, but I often get compliments on my special style.

Of course, being unique is not just about the outside— it's what's inside as well. One of the coolest compliments I've received was when someone said to me, "Most women try to be different and like to be told they are different. But you really *are* different!"

It all comes back to embracing who you truly are, which can be very difficult. I bet everyone reading this knows at least five people who are unsatisfied with their jobs. But they stay for the money, the benefits, and what they think is security. Truth is, these people are cheating themselves in the long run.

Not long ago, I spent some time working at a magazine. At first, I really loved the job. I did well and was elevated to a higher title. But when I brought my creative, non-conforming ideas to meetings, they were shunned. It was frustrating because I had so much more to offer than what I was permitted to do. The job became stifling, so I got out.

Immediately afterward, I felt refreshed and ready for the next chapter in my life. I was ecstatic that I was no longer living a lie by going to a job I'd quickly outgrown. I could have remained safe, stayed on board, and been a people pleaser. It's so easy to play the game. But that's not me. There are no guarantees in life, and I want to live each day being the happiest I can be. Even if I must take a temporary setback to get to the next level in life, I will go for it.

It's a fact that people who don't lose don't win, either. Failing is just as important as succeeding, because that's when you grow the most. And whether you are succeeding or failing, the opinions of other people should not matter. It's your life, not theirs!

So, if you want to quit your corporate job to live on an island and sell fruit, do it! Keeping up with the Joneses is a thing of the past. More and more people are celebrating their uniqueness instead of hiding in the shadow of a life that might make their parents proud but makes them unhappy. Having the power to think independently is one of the most unique and rewarding things a person can do.

In fact, if you take your uniqueness into a professional setting, you can capitalize on being distinct. Being exclusive can give you a competitive edge in the workforce. After all, in the marketplace, if others are providing the same benefits you are, there's no reason for you to be there too. There's value in being rare. You want to be the one who is first in the field.

Imagine being at an important company meeting. Suppose that instead of brainstorming, everyone went in with the same ideas. The meeting wouldn't be much of a success, would it? Triumphant ideas are singular ones.

Sometimes we can get down on ourselves if we feel—and know—we're different from others. We can feel isolated or even rejected. But following the pack leads to mediocrity. Using your uniqueness to your advantage is something to be embraced, especially if others are challenging your ideas and believing that you are wrong and that you'll fail.

People who are different are a breath of fresh air. Standing out from the mainstream makes them interesting, and they lead by example.

Are you someone who knows you are different but you're currently feeling trapped? There are concrete steps to take to be yourself and shine. The first thing to do is seek out others who also might be in your shoes and/or who understand and respect that you are not like everyone else. If it takes a while to find others like you, there's nothing wrong with being alone for the time being. If you like your own company, you won't really feel lonely. When you start coming out of your shell and expressing your true self, you might even find yourself drifting apart from people, including your family. That's okay. As a human being, you have the right to be who you truly are. And that's exactly how you should view others: as human beings who have the right to be who they truly are, too. So, stop comparing yourself to them.

If anyone wants to judge you for how you think or how you look, they just don't get it. Don't allow their opinions to hold you back from being yourself.

Each day, make it a point to practice embracing your true, unique self. For example, say your friends are going to a movie that really doesn't interest you. Don't go! It's that simple. Instead, go to the movie *you* want to see, even if it means going alone. Or do something else you would rather do. Or just stay home. You have choices, and when you do it your way, you'll always come up a winner.

Next time you decide you want to change your hair, don't ask your friends for their advice. Just go to the salon and do what *you* want. You're the one who looks in the mirror every day. If there's something new you want to try, go for it! Your opinions and desires are the only ones that matter.

When it comes to doing new things and taking chances—whether personal or professional—the only thing stopping you is you. Going out on a limb can yield some pretty great benefits. For instance, you might meet new friends when you attend a fitness class or other event alone.

Who knows where life can lead you when you're being true to yourself. A new hobby could turn into a career. You might meet someone special just because you're grabbing a bite to eat by yourself. You never know, because the possibilities are endless.

Now, there is nothing wrong with joining and fitting in, if that's how you truly feel and if that's what you genuinely want and enjoy. Whatever you do or say or buy, having a passion behind it is what makes it a valid, enriching choice. Look at yourself before looking at others. And ask yourself things like, *Do I really want this? Do I really stand by what I'm going to say, or am I saying it just to fit in?*

By being true to yourself and embracing your own uniqueness, people will remember you. Think back to the snowboarding amputee, Amy Purdy. Another reason her live testimony made me cry was because she reminded me of my late grandmother, who lost a leg from the knee down because of diabetes. My grandmother's passion for life was extraordinary. Even with one leg, she traveled, went on roller coasters, and flirted with Elvis impersonators. When she died, we buried her wearing an Elvis watch. And there were so many people at her funeral, you'd have thought it was a celebrity who had passed. All my life people told me, "Your grandmother is cool." She truly was. When I was a teenager, she was able to keep up with me in conversation about pop culture. She was always joking around; she even joked about losing her leg!

She could laugh about anything and enjoy herself in any situation. Not only was she at peace with who she was, but she loved living the life that was authentic to her—no matter what anyone else might have thought about it.

My grandmother was not a celebrity like Amy Purdy, but she is nevertheless a perfect example of how each and every one of us can embrace uniqueness, even during rough times.

chapter four

(BE)EMOTIONAL

As a member of Generation X, I have to say that honesty is what I love most about younger generations. I grew up in a time when it was perceived as shameful to share a family secret or let people see you cry. It was a weakness to allow your flaws to be visible, and it was frowned upon to express yourself. You always had to be strong—or at least put on a façade that you were. This went for both men and women.

Then something changed in the 1990s. It became okay to admit you had problems. Young people were not shy about going to therapy and taking antidepressant medications. The book *Prozac Nation* by Elizabeth Wurtzel, published in 1994, was a big hit that seemed to give people permission to be open about their struggles and how they were getting through them.

Gen X people paved the way for younger generations to embrace honesty and emotions. During the 1990s, when I was cultivating my writing and poetry skills and hanging out with other like-minded creative types, one of my male friends told me why he believed in always being real. "If you keep skeletons in the closet," he said, "you'll always have to remember which skeleton is in which closet. It's so much easier to just be honest."

I agreed. It's not only easier to be truthful, it's also refreshing. Being both authentic and sometimes emotional sets the stage for great relationships. To speak freely and speak the truth is a commitment to the soul; it takes guts.

Sometimes people lie because they want you to like them. But then it backfires. When people are caught in lies, it creates distrust. Then it's hard to move forward, whether in a friendship or a romance.

But it's not easy to come from a place of honesty. There are always those who are around to pass judgment. So, we are taking a big chance by being emotional and speaking from our hearts. Nevertheless, by doing this, we are being whole. Not lying to others also means not lying to ourselves.

When we deny our real feelings, we live a lie. Therefore, our relationships are also lies. Sometimes people can get caught up in living a fantasy. In a relationship, they can get involved with someone who is emotionally unavailable, yet they continue for months, even years, as if nothing is wrong. Deep down, one might hope that by suppressing their emotions, the other person eventually will come around. That won't work, though, because there will never be a high level of intimacy if a relationship is based on lies and avoidance. It's a lose-lose situation. By dodging the risk of saying something like, "Hey, this really isn't what I want," and working on building a better relationship, you're missing out on so much. Wouldn't it be better to have a connection built on true emotions? That is the only path to something rich, joyful, meaningful, and lasting. The best relationships are based on honesty.

Nirvana's Kurt Cobain once said, "I'd rather be hated for who I am than loved for who I'm not."

I agree wholeheartedly. I can't even imagine putting on a mask and having people love me for being fake. So, I take the risk of honesty, and sometimes it's difficult. Here's an example: For many years, I was a vegetarian. Then a few years ago, with the advice of a nutritionist, I added some grass-fed beef into my diet on occasion. I had to tell my vegetarian friends; I didn't want them to continue to identify with me as a vegetarian, because that wouldn't have been the truth. Believe it or not, some of them stopped talking to me! I was shocked by the judgment.

You can't always predict how people will react to your honesty, but those who respond negatively probably weren't meant to be your friends. It can be hard to face that reality, but it's more valuable to live with integrity than to live with a false sense of security. And for as hurtful as it can be to share your truths with the wrong people, it can be a beautiful treasure to find the right people with whom to share your deepest emotions. When two or more people connect over something serious and real, that bond can rock your world.

It's important that as you work to operate in an authentic fashion, you develop a thick skin. It takes hard work to fully believe in yourself and what you are about, no matter what someone else says. The good news is, you can build your self-esteem in just ten minutes a day by watching self-help or inspirational videos while you have your morning coffee. It also can be helpful to keep a journal of affirmations, goals, and achievements and to make a weekly list of the great things in your life. Occasionally, you still might fall back into old patterns of self-doubt, but if you practice these things faithfully (even when it seems counterintuitive), you will develop a ton of confidence. You'll be able to accept the fact that not everyone is going to like you, and that will be a great relief! Being able to be true to yourself without worrying what others think is so rewarding. When that happens, you won't let a snarky comment on social media get you down. You won't mourn the loss of a fake friend, either.

The thing you must remember is that when people genuinely care about you, they might not like *everything* about you, but that won't stop them from loving you. Nobody is perfect. The friends who stay are the ones who are willing to work out arguments, disagree without being disagreeable, and love you even if you disagree over things of great importance.

In a mature relationship, it's okay to fight. It all depends on *how* you fight. I have a very good longtime friend with whom I fight from time to time. In the middle of our arguments, we might both be crying, but we'll say things like, "I love you and I know we will work this out." No wonder we've been friends since we were teenagers. We trust each other, and we know it's okay to be completely honest and open with each other.

Another key point to remember: How people react is about *them*, not about *you*. Someone might blow up at you because he or she is having a bad day and is upset about something else entirely. You can't control how people think, feel, or behave, so it's best just to be who you are. You can't live life walking on eggshells.

Of course, you can be thoughtful in how, when, and where you share your opinions and feelings. We all know there are certain topics that aren't appropriate for certain company. It's a matter of knowing and respecting your audience. Sometimes, it's best to avoid touchy subjects, such as politics or religion. But you should always feel comfortable sharing your dreams, successes, and failures with the people in your circle of friends. You never know when you might inspire someone or meet a new friend.

A couple years ago, I interviewed a teacher for a local newspaper. About a year later, he asked me to be a speaker at his school. I was thrilled for the opportunity and for his kind words. In his message to me, he wrote: "I've followed you on Facebook for over a year. You're very positive, but not only about yourself. You are positive to other people too."

I truly believe that the more honest and emotional we are, the easier it is to be positive. When you let yourself get emotional, it's a beautiful release. After a good cry, you can go to bed and wake up to the start of a new day. But if you hold it in, there will come a point at which you explode. Pent-up emotions might lead you to say things you don't mean and ultimately regret.

It's been scientifically proven that crying can help you feel better. It's certainly not something to be embarrassed about. Crying is a sign that you're strong, because vulnerability comes from great strength. Letting go means you are confident enough not to care what others think.

After a good cry, you might feel more energetic and more positive about facing your challenges. So, don't be embarrassed, and don't apologize either.

To be able to cry when you need to and to express yourself as you need to takes practice. It's not easy to be the real you 24/7, because not everyone else is. It might take a long time to meet a kindred spirit when it comes to honesty. And trust me, it is disappointing to try to become friends with someone who isn't as emotionally giving as you are. The thing is, you need to give people a chance to warm up to you. Just because you're open and expressive, you can't expect everyone else to be like you. Do forgive new friends for telling white lies instead of sharing their true opinions. Eventually, once trust is built, they will come around.

While being honest and expressive around your friends is a great way to build trust, applying emotions in the workplace is a bit tricky. Whereas people you choose to be around—friends and loved ones—understand where you're coming from, co-workers might not. Co-workers and managers might view emotions differently. Some might understand your perspective, but some might not want to rock the boat. That's why EQ is a big thing in the work world.

EQ is emotional intelligence. Having a high EQ in the workplace can lead to promotions and better opportunities. People with a high EQ don't put down others, and they don't lose their cool. They understand their strengths and weaknesses and can relate to and respect the strengths and weaknesses of others. They know how to advocate for themselves without being rude or defensive, and they know how to empower others by helping them grow.

My motto has always been, "I'm great, you're great—let's be great together!" When co-workers share that mind-set, it makes for a fantastic team. It also facilitates communication, because everyone is working toward the same goal in a positive way.

Yet, people with a high EQ don't necessarily avoid conflict. They know how to address problems head-on. They see challenging conversations as a way to build trust and actually strengthen relationships.

Many years ago, while I still worked in corporate, I was harassed in the workplace. I was young, so I did lose my cool, but I was smart enough to lose it behind closed doors, venting to management. I was told by my manager that I could feel free to vent to him any time. It was a relief to express myself to someone who listened, but the harassment continued. My next step was HR. Speaking up for myself in an intelligent way was the right thing to do, and the timing was perfect. It just so happened there was another position in the company, on another floor, for more pay. It was my first official promotion. I took the position and ended up staying with the company another year before I left to pursue more creative endeavors.

So, what does that say about a person with a high EQ? You *can* speak up when you're hurting. You don't have to hold in negativity. Done wisely, it can produce great results. Emotion at work conveys your passion for the job when you express yourself productively and constructively. A good boss or supervisor will see that and appreciate it.

Though sometimes a person who rocks the boat isn't the most popular one in the group, that person could be the one who truly makes a difference in the world. Your unique vision could be a positive one for not only you but for your friends, family, and work team.

Take, for example, Dr. Martin Luther King Jr. Yes, he was a great leader because he was smart, determined, and confident. He was also a great leader because he used his pain and sadness to fuel his mission and to connect to others. He used equal parts emotion and intellect to appeal to the hearts and minds of America. His "I Have a Dream" speech, of course, is a grand part of history, his words and delivery conveying such deep emotion. Where would the United States be if Dr. King hadn't been willing not only to say, but to *show*, what was in his heart?

Always remember that your ideas matter. And in return, you can be supportive of someone else who goes against the grain. Giving someone a chance to shine is a wonderful thing. Courageous people can move mountains together! You can teach others that it's a great idea to be outspoken and try new things.

Expressing your emotions makes you a better person, a better employee, a better friend, and a better partner. When you're authentic, you shine because you feel whole and at peace.

Make a point to be as expressive about the good as you are about the bad. Once you start telling a friend your problems, it's easy to get carried away. So, take a moment to also think about the good things in your life. Don't be afraid to be just as emotive when talking about your highs, successes, and the fun things you do in life.

Just as there should be no shame in tears of sadness, there should be no shame in tears of joy. If something great has happened in your life, you should be able to share with a select group of people without fear they'll be resentful or jealous of you. It takes courage to share sad things, or speak your mind at a meeting, and it also takes courage to share something amazing. So, the same rules apply. Seek out people you can trust to love you for who you truly are, whether you're feeling sad, motivated, or on top of the world.

You matter. Your feelings matter. And you have every right to be *you*!

chapter five

(BE)GENEROUS

Nobody can deny how wonderful it feels to be generous. Every simple act of kindness—such as paying it forward and picking up the tab for someone or throwing a few bucks in a donation can for sheltered animals—helps to make a difference.

When I was waitressing, there was a customer who frequently would pick up the check for people she didn't know. Whenever you'd give her the bill, she'd point to a random table and say, "I'll take their check too." It was usually an elderly couple she selected, and it made their day.

And about a year ago, a friend was struggling with health issues. When he put up a Go Fund Me page, I was thankful I was able to make a decent-sized donation. And to help even further, I commissioned his artist wife to paint a gift for my mother's birthday.

Stories like this, the gift of treasure, are endless. We all have them. It's human nature to want to help others. Just think of the old saying: "It is better to give than to receive."

But giving doesn't always have to be about money. There are also the gifts of time and talent.

My mother was a generous woman. But as a single, working mom, she wasn't always around. She gave me so many material things when I was small, but the one thing I wanted more than anything else was her time. So, when I heard the bathtub water running at night, I knew she'd be in there a while. I'd go into the bathroom, sit on the toilet seat, and talk to her while she relaxed in the tub. I had her undivided attention—the gift of time— and it was a true mother-daughter bonding experience.

When my mother wasn't around, my grandmother was. Many of her good qualities rubbed off on me, including generosity. Every year on Labor Day weekend, we loved to "stay up and watch the stars come out" on the Jerry Lewis MDA Labor Day Telethon that benefitted the Muscular Dystrophy Association. My grandmother would donate each year. When I started working, I contributed to the cause as well. Then I took it a step further. I organized several poetry readings to benefit the MDA. Other poets and I used our time and talents to raise money, and art galleries and coffee shops were generous enough to let us use their facilities. They didn't take any money from us; they hosted our events out of the kindness of their hearts.

A few years after my grandmother died of diabetes complications, I was a DJ at The Knitting Factory in New York City at an event to benefit diabetes research. The event was a blow-out, with several DJs and bands performing both upstairs and downstairs. Some of the bands were well-known, but others were struggling artists who didn't make much money. Still, they donated their time and didn't get paid for the gig.

Studies have shown that being generous reduces blood pressure and stress. That makes sense, because when we give, we feel a sense of purpose. It's a great feeling to know you are needed. I've learned that giving helps lift me up when I'm feeling my worst. Doing something nice for someone, even if it's something small like giving a "like" on a Facebook post to help someone promote his or her business, will raise your spirits.

Generosity is not something to be taken for granted. My husband, Dennis, is such a giver, always doing something special for me. So, I make it a point to surprise him with an unexpected concert ticket or random love notes around the house. People always say, "It's the little things in life." They are right!

Not only can generosity make a marriage stronger, but it also can build better bonds in friendships. We'll naturally feel closer to those who are kind enough to reach out with a phone call instead of a brief text message. It will put a bigger smile on our face if we receive a hand-written thank-you note instead of an email or social media message. And how about those friends who can commit to making a lunch date rather than saying, "We'll have to get together someday."

Generous friends inspire us to be more giving ourselves. When they give to the charities we support, we are there to give back to theirs. When they support our dreams, we support theirs. It's always a win-win.

It's worth noting that the more we support each other, the more opportunities become available to us. For example, one of my friends started a home-based business taking care of dogs. She told me I'd inspired her because I work for myself as a freelance journalist and author. Now her business is thriving. Before she started her business, she saw on Facebook that a local restaurant owner needed help writing a book. She contacted me immediately, and I scored the gig!

Generosity keeps paying back and paying back and paying back. It's a snowball effect you can't deny. Blessings might come from anywhere when you're of a giving mind-set.

One summer, there was a terrible story in the news about a cat that was assaulted on the Fourth of July. The cat, named Katy, survived the attack, but her tail had to be amputated. Even without her tail, she was still a beauty. Hundreds of people, including myself, poured their hearts out sending donations. Hundreds, including myself, also expressed interest in adopting Katy once she healed and the shelter released her. Finally, at the end of the summer, she was adopted. People continued to give money to benefit the cat for future medical bills.

So many compassionate, loving people bonded and became cheerleaders for the health of this pretty cat. Some people even said they were adopting a cat in honor of Katy. While all this was happening, a feral cat started coming around my home, so my husband and I took him in. A month later, I won a six-month supply of cat food from a company that freeze-dries raw product, all because I shared the story of taking in a feral who had feline immunodeficiency virus.

That's how the chain of kindness works. People help one another; they're generous with money, with kind thoughts, with time. And it comes back in a beautiful circle. Just thinking about it sends chills up my spine (and maybe even brings a tear to my eye). People are always attracted to givers. One person starts giving, and then someone else hops onboard and gives, as well.

No matter what our net worth is, there's always someone with less who could use our help. If we don't have money to spare, we can always give away our old clothes, shoes, and even books.

What matters most is our intent—the spirit of love and kindness behind our actions. Some time ago, I was assigned to report on a senior Valentine's Day dance at a fancy banquet hall with valet parking. As I was leaving, someone gave me a heart-shaped box filled with chocolates. When I got outside, I realized I didn't have cash on me to tip the guy who had parked my car. So, I gave him my Valentine's chocolates and said, "Happy Valentine's Day." The happy look on his face was priceless! In hindsight, I realize I could have gone back inside to the ATM for some cash, but I was in a hurry on deadline and not thinking. Nevertheless, my heart was in the right place—and I think that box of chocolates made the guy happier than cash would have! Just a simple act of kindness goes a long way.

A professional setting offers countless opportunities to exhibit generosity. Mentoring, for example, is a way to share your time and experience with a new or junior co-worker, paying forward the wisdom someone probably passed onto you early in your career. Take the new person out for coffee or lunch and share your time as a friend; or, if the person reports to you, consider creating a formal mentorship process that shows you're invested in your team member's success, both now and into the future.

Similarly, being generous with praise is a perfect way to build morale and keep your teammates motivated. You don't have to be someone's supervisor to tell her she does a good job or to encourage him during a difficult project. Work is such a big part of all our lives; helping people feel good about themselves at the office can make a giant impact on their self-esteem and overall sense of well-being. And let's not forget to state the obvious: When you're free and easy with giving genuine compliments that show you've been paying attention, in return you'll gain a reputation for being a collaborative teammate. That certainly won't hurt your career!

Every day, everywhere we are, there are so many creative ways to be generous. I've heard people say they like to do things such as leaving cash in random places in dollar stores. If you're on a tight budget, you can always leave a kind message in a random place. One day I decided to write twenty-three—because it was the twenty-third of the month—positive messages on small pieces of paper. They read things like, "You are loved," "You're awesome!" and "You are blessed!" I put them in a small pouch and carried them with me throughout the day. That night, I was at a Sheila E. concert. Sheila began to preach the word of love and encouraged people to hug a stranger and shake hands with one another. It was then that I remembered my happy messages. I handed them out to people around me, and in return I received so many smiles from strangers. I still had some left over at the end of the concert, so I put them on cars as I walked through the parking lot. Handing out my messages made me feel at least as good as it did the people who received my notes.

You also can be generous by doing something nice for someone in secret. This has happened to me a few times, and it feels great to know someone is thinking of you and wants to bless you for no particular reason. Admittedly, I drove myself a little crazy trying to figure out who had done these nice things for me, but the best advice I received was, "Just enjoy your gift."

By giving anonymously, these generous givers were delivering in the best way possible—without the expectation of receiving something in return. Giving is fulfilling. Knowing you did something nice that made someone very happy can leave you feeling warm and satisfied.

Last year, right before the holiday season, *USA Today* ran an article on some of the celebrity secret Santas. Actor Mark Ruffalo shared Starbucks gift cards with his online followers and encouraged others to do the same. In response, Robert Downey Jr. and Zendaya did just that. And Tyler Perry paid off $434,000 worth of layaway items at two Atlanta-area Walmart stores. He announced what he did in an Instagram video, which inspired others to help too. A day later, Kid Rock followed Perry's lead and paid off the layaway at a Walmart in Nashville, Tennessee. His totals came to about $81,000.

Even if you're not a superstar, you can feel like one when you do something to brighten another's day. You might not get a spot on the Hollywood Walk of Fame, but your kindness surely will be remembered.

One of the world's best-known givers was Princess Diana. She first caught the public eye as a fashion trend-setter, but her charity work is her real legacy.

Princess Diana contributed to more than 100 charities. She also gave of her time, visiting schools and hospitals. She changed the world's view on HIV and AIDS when she visited AIDS patients at a hospital in London in 1987. There's a famous photo of the princess shaking hands with a patient without wearing gloves, an act that defied the false belief that HIV or AIDS could be spread merely by touch. The image truly illustrates Diana's genuine love for mankind. And she made a difference, because she helped dispel baseless fears that have largely ceased to exist today. Princess Diana educated people— that's certainly a gift!

In addition to shaking hands with the AIDS patient without gloves, Princess Diana took it a step further, breaking the royal protocol and ceasing to wear gloves completely. Why? She loved direct human contact with those she met during her charitable and public engagements.

In a time when everyone is so phone-obsessed, the world certainly could use a bit more "reach out and touch someone" enthusiasm. How often do you greet a new neighbor with a welcome basket of baked goods or cleaning supplies for their new home? In fact, many people don't even take time to get to know the individuals and families living around them. Personally, I feel very blessed to live across the street from a woman who will take it upon herself to bring in my Amazon packages if I've been gone all day.

Sometimes, when I'm in a business situation and someone goes to shake my hand, I'll respond with a hug instead. People love this! In other cultures, people greet by kissing both cheeks. We truly need to bring back the human touch. If you are shy, this can be challenging, but try to take baby steps toward coming out of your shell.

For instance, when you're in a supermarket, be conscious of those around you. Don't be in such a rush to get in and get out. Make it an experience. Smile at people. Let someone go ahead of you in line. Help an elderly person reach for something. These are all ways you can be generous without spending a dime. If you do happen to have some extra cash on hand, you can always pay for someone else's groceries.

Being generous, in any way you can, puts you in a great mind-set. You're happier, calmer, more forgiving, and more enthusiastic about life in general. Generosity doesn't take much. But what it gives back can be monumental.

chapter six

(BE)KIND

Acts of kindness—whether you give them or receive them—can turn negatives into positives and completely alter the mood of a day.

Kindness goes deeper than just niceness. It's a mix of generosity, thoughtfulness, openness, patience, compassion, and empathy. It's more than being polite (though there's certainly nothing wrong with being polite!). And the good news is, acts of kindness are all around us when we look for them and when we strive to touch the lives of others.

Sometimes it could be a complete stranger who makes our day—and in the strangest way. Once, I was walking out of the Port Authority and a homeless man asked me for money. Now, this was back in the late 1980s when New York City was grittier and tougher. If I'd reached into my pocketbook, there was a chance the man would have grabbed it from me. So, I simply told him I didn't have money to give him.

"You come to a big city like this without money?" he replied.

"I'm going to work. I just have enough money with me to buy lunch," I said.

"Not even a penny?" he asked.

"No, not even a penny," I responded.

With that, he reached into his own pocket and took out a handful of pennies. "Nobody should be without pennies," he said, handing me some coins.

Not wanting to hurt his feelings, I took the pennies and thanked him. It's amazing how someone with so little could be so kind. Whether he was sincere or a little unhinged, he certainly put a smile on my face and gave me some things to think about.

Another time, also in New York, a homeless person asked me for a dime. I gave him a quarter and he a gave me fifteen cents change! That was priceless—and precious.

And when I used to work in Hoboken, New Jersey, I'd pass a young homeless couple on the streets almost every day. My heart bled for them because it seemed like they were truly making an effort to find a job. Some people just get bad breaks in life. Each day, I'd take some time to chat with them and they'd tell me about their job searches or how good it felt when they collected enough money to pay for a shower at the YMCA. Their eyes would light up if they spoke about a job interview coming up. I made sure I always had a dollar to give them. One day when I gave a dollar, the girl gave me a cute pin with a turtle on it. The pin wasn't worth much, but the fact that this homeless girl was giving *me* something back truly warmed my heart. The way she smiled as she pinned the turtle on my jacket was worth a million dollars.

Everyone has treasured moments like these that will always stand out in our memories. When you think of experiences like this, you can't help but beam. The world is really a wonderful place when you think of all the angels who are out there, coming right into your world when you least expect them—and probably when you most need them.

Little things go a long way. Are there standout moments in your life when someone made your day by a simple act of kindness? Are you doing similar things for others? If not, it's never too late to start. In the course of a day, there are many opportunities for kindness. Have patience while in line for a bank teller. If someone dials your number by mistake, don't get frustrated; wish them a nice day instead. Make a small donation to charity. For example, sometimes I'll make a vow to donate to the first fund-raising campaign that comes up in my Facebook feed.

With our busy, high-pressure lives these days, it can be easy to become focused on ourselves, keeping up a hectic pace and trying to balance seemingly endless to-do lists. I've found that keeping a giving journal helps keep me on track by reminding me to be generous, thoughtful, and caring.

Most of us have heard of keeping gratitude journals—recording the good things in life for which we're thankful. A giving journal can be a great complement. I keep my giving journal in a place where I can see it, so I'm always conscious of it. I make two columns for each page. One column is to record my act of kindness; in the other, I describe the reactions of those affected by my acts. If you wish, you can add a third column to note how great giving made *you* feel.

My giving journal inspires me to keep reaching out and putting more good into the world. It challenges me to stay kind no matter how I'm feeling or what might be going on with me. And when I'm down in the dumps and feeling unworthy, my journal reminds me of the good things I do and the efforts I'm making to be the best person I can be.

When I look back at my life, I'm always thankful I've kept journals because they let me revisit all the good, kind things others have done for me. Some things you never want to forget. For instance, in high school I was being bullied by a group of kids. A girl named Pam stood up for me and put them in their place. I was too shy to thank her back then, but years later I looked her up on Facebook. She agreed to let me buy her lunch. I also gave her a plant to express my gratitude—even though decades had passed! Her act of extraordinary kindness was, to me, also an act of extraordinary courage and love. It let me know I had an ally in the world at a time when I felt very alone.

More recently, when I was going through a trying

time, my friend Joan gave me a beautiful, stylish salmon-colored shawl and said the sweetest thing: "Just put it around you when you're sad, and think of me hugging you." Amazing! Just what I needed to hear.

When I first started dating my husband, I was no longer happy working as a newspaper journalist. He knew it was rough for me to get through the day, so he'd buy gifts for me ahead of time. Then, when I expressed I was having an especially hard day, he'd surprise me with a book or a piece of jewelry. Always remember: You don't need a special occasion to express how much you care for someone.

When kindness begins small, it seems like other opportunities to be kind present themselves. There's always someone around who needs help. You might have a friend who needs to vent; being a good listener is a powerful gift. Or maybe you have an older relative who can't see too well and doesn't like to drive in the dark; it would be a great help if you offered a lift for that person in the evening hours. You can even be kind to the earth by picking up litter and making an effort to recycle. And consider getting a pet from a shelter instead of from a breeder. All these things add up to make the world a better place for all of us.

And isn't that what heroes do? When I think of my heroes, I think of anyone who operates on a higher plane and knows we're put on earth for a reason: to be the change we want to see.

I'm blessed to have so many of these types of people in my life. They're people who are motivated to do great things. They're givers, not takers. They elevate others instead of slandering and gossiping.

It makes the news when celebrities do good deeds, but there are so many everyday extraordinary people in our own neighborhoods. Seek them out, make them your friends, and watch how they make you smile and inspire you to open your own heart.

As you begin to change and grow, you might see that you drift from old friends and start attracting new people who are more like the new you. You'll be much happier for it. What's even cooler is that these amazing people will start to see *you* as someone who inspires them and makes them better humans. How extraordinary is that?!

chapter seven

(BE)WEIRD

The thing about being weird is that you don't realize you are weird until someone else points it out to you. Your "weirdness" comes from the inside; it's what sets you apart from others.

As a child, I saw other children as ordinary. I didn't want to be like them. I wanted to be like the adults. And why not? I grew up in a time when adults, and even teenagers, were incredibly exciting: the 1970s. This was a time when people expressed themselves very creatively: bell-bottom pants, long hair, turquoise jewelry, red nails, and mini-skirts.

Like many other little girls of my generation, I wanted to be Cher, so I grew my hair super long. Then, as a preteen, I discovered Freddie Mercury.

One of my friends told me my motto should be "Dare to be different."

But I questioned the word "dare." Being different was natural to me. It didn't feel like I was doing something daring. I was just being myself.

This particular "friend" gave me such a hard time growing up. She criticized everything I did that she considered different. When she started high school, she left me behind, and it took me years to realize the problem was her, not me.

There's no reason to hang out with people who don't let you embrace who you really are. There are plenty of people who will. You just need to find them. For me, one of my best friendships—with Joan, whom I mentioned earlier—began when I was a senior in high school. Joan was a year younger than I. We connected over our love for music, and she liked the fact that I was different and stood out. I was then dressing like a punk rocker, with ripped jeans, heavy eye makeup, Converse All-Star sneakers, and spiked hair. Joan started wearing spiked bracelets like I did. We were the ring leaders of a group of fellow punk rockers who started having record parties and going to concerts together. This formed the foundation of my understanding that I could be who I wanted to be and people would still like me.

If you look for them, you will find your fellow weirdos. First, you have to let go of the negative people in your life. High school is the perfect time for that realization, but if it takes a little longer, that's okay—you have your entire life ahead of you.

Years after high school, I was humbled when Joan said something very kind about me. "I always feel comfortable around you," she said. "I can gain weight or have a pimple and you still make me feel beautiful."

It's true that when we feel good about ourselves, we

naturally make others feel good too. But that can happen only when we are 100 percent happy with who and how we are—even if it means being a weirdo.

So, what exactly is a weirdo? You could define it as someone who is eccentric, odd, nonconformist, or free-spirited. But I like to see it as simply being an individual.

Freddie Mercury will always be the weirdo I connect with. His extravagant confidence is what set him apart from the crowd. But there are thousands of other weirdos out there who might resonate with you. Take Prince, who once dropped the "Prince" moniker in favor of an unpronounceable glyph (which led people to call him "The Artist Formerly Known as Prince"). He changed his look numerous times, and his sound was a mix of rock, soul, funk, and pop—something truly unmatched by other artists.

There's also actress Helena Bonham Carter, whose costume-styled fashion sense frequently lands her on both best- and worst-dressed lists. Regardless of what she wears, she's had a successful acting career for decades.

Several years ago, there was a contestant on "America's Next Top Model" whom I'll never forget. Her name was Allison Harvard. Her eyes were huge and doll-like, and she had a fascination with blood and thought nose-bleeds were pretty. She lost the competition, but her uniqueness made her unforgettable.

The list of people in the media who are considered weird can go on forever. As long as someone's weirdness isn't hurting anyone, there's really no problem with it. As my grandmother once said, "If people are talking about you, they are leaving someone else alone." Be who you are; it's nobody's else's business.

Weird people make the world go 'round. Those with creative minds can tune in to everything around them; it's the key to their creativity. Average people react to situations based on what they have been taught. A weird person goes against the grain. He or she is less likely to listen to authority or understand the "rules" of society. Therefore, creatives live in a world that is more fluid. They are unconventional. They ask lots of questions— some would say too many. But being weird is what allows them to have a creative breakthrough.

No one would have predicted that a musical about Founding Father Alexander Hamilton would become a smash Broadway hit...nor that it would be largely rapped...nor that it would star a cast of non-white performers. But that was Lin-Manuel Miranda's weird vision, and now *Hamilton* is an award-winning household name, loved by both adults and kids who otherwise might barely know anything about the first U.S. Secretary of the Treasury.

Honky Tonk musician Sierra Ferrell is another one blazing her own trail. She's a contradiction of styles, with her septum ring, vintage country dresses and a tattoo near her eye. Some people have to go online and criticize what they don't understand, but I find her chic fashion sense inspiring! In fact, her unique style drew me to her music in the first place. Then I got hooked on her music and talked my husband into driving two hours to see her live. The next thing I knew, she had a record deal—septum ring and all.

Embracing your inner weirdo takes guts; it's a matter of learning how to be yourself. You'd think we're all born knowing how to do exactly that, but somewhere along the way, we get the message from society that we should be invisible, that we need to blend in with the crowd. It often happens without our even noticing. We stop seeing our true selves, and consequently, no one else sees the real us, either.

Some time ago, I kept having the strangest experience and I couldn't figure out why. Whenever I was in a grocery store, at least one person would hit me with his or her cart. My husband even noticed it. He'd say, "You're such a small target—why do people keep banging into you?"

He even noted that someone could be going in a totally different direction with a cart, then veer right over toward me—like a bowling ball with an incredible curve. It never failed. Right toward me and then *bang*! Then I'd start yelling, and they'd start apologizing. This happened almost every time I went to the supermarket. It got to a point where I considered hiring someone to do my grocery shopping.

Strangely, once I started dying my hair brilliant shades of red and purple, people stopped banging their carts into me. I can't imagine how a simple thing such as changing your hair color can make such a difference in how people react to you. Do people now *see* me because my hair stands out? Perhaps.

You see, as I approached fifty, I began to dress more conservatively and let my heavily highlighted hair go back to its natural brown color. Thinking back, I admit I looked a bit on the mousy side. But the truth is, I'm not a mousy kind of person. I have a dynamic, bubbly personality, with a unique way about me. I'd always dressed to suit my personality, from my punk-rock days, to my goth stage with crimson hair and black undertones, to wearing the same purple, rubber dress Heather Locklear wore on the cover of *Details* magazine in the 1990s. I'd always prided myself on being a head-turner when it came to fashion.

What had changed?

I thought that as a middle-aged woman I should be a certain way. But whose way is that? It's not *my* way. Nor is it the way of my friends, who are all middle-aged, stylish, standout types. None of them is invisible, so why should I be?

In order to feel like *me* again, I went back to doing things as I used to: wearing ripped jeans, high-heeled shoes, and girly dresses, and yes, dying my hair odd colors. I even got my first tattoo in two decades.

Young women at my bank began praising me for my

style. I started getting respect I'd craved for years. And I can honestly say, people don't bang their carts into me anymore. Instead, they stop and talk to me.

When I think of this, I regret that I ever stopped being true to myself. I let misconceptions about aging change the way I behaved. But now, I let my appearance reflect the energy that shines from within.

Don't let perceptions—or misperceptions—stand in the way of being who you really are. You can read all the "rules" you want, but if you're not feeling it, there's absolutely no reason to go by the book. And it's not just about aging. We've been trained to believe moms should look and act a certain way; men wear this and women wear that; and professionals always need to be buttoned-up and formal. The truth is, many of those walls are coming down. Though there's a time and a place for following old-school norms, there's an increasing openness to doing what feels right and authentic to each individual.

And thank goodness! If we cover up what makes us weird, how will we find our weirdo tribe?

You see, not fitting in is never the problem. The problem is trying to fit in with people who don't get you. I won't lie and say I never felt a little sad about not fitting in with certain groups. But then I remember, it's like trying to get a toothpaste cap on a ketchup bottle. It just doesn't work. And fitting in wouldn't have made me happy in the long run. The grass is not always greener when you have to stifle yourself to be like others.

It's ironic, but sometimes getting out of your social comfort zone is actually what enables you to become more comfortable with yourself. If you're spending your time trying to look or act "right" for a certain group of people in your neighborhood, school, or workplace, you probably can sense in your heart that things aren't the way they're meant to be.

So, that might mean you spend more time alone for a while, getting to know yourself and better understanding the real you. Or, it might mean you break out and introduce yourself to new people, places, and experiences as you work to find the right fit. If someone you know thinks knitting, gaming, working out, etc., isn't cool, who really cares? Move on from that person, spend time doing what you love, and you'll attract and be attracted to others with similar "weird" interests.

One of the great inspirations in media today is Jazz Jennings. Jennings is a YouTube personality, model, and LGBT rights activist. She is also one of the youngest publicly documented people to identify as transgender. Jennings was assigned male at birth, but as soon as she could speak, she made it clear she was female. Jennings received national attention in 2007 when her interview with Barbara Walters aired on "20/20." She also hosted a series of YouTube videos about her life, titled "I Am Jazz." In 2013, she founded Purple Rainbow Tails, a company whose proceeds support transgender children.

Jazz Jennings is a prime example of the fact when you don't let anything stand in the way of being your true self, you can make a great difference for other people, as well. She has said, "When I leave, I want the world to be in a better state than when I arrived."

When you allow yourself to be *you*, it means you've stopped judging yourself. And that's when the magic happens in your life. You meet the people who will be your lifelong friends; you discover the hobbies and activities that feed your soul; and you find the career track that ignites your passion.

Being different is a gift. And it's one we all have inside of us if we're brave enough to unwrap the box and let ourselves be real. How others see us should not stop us from being the happiest we can be. And the only way we can do that is by not lying to ourselves. We owe it to ourselves to be true to our beautiful, weird selves.

chapter eight

(BE)OPEN

When I think of being open, the first thing that comes to mind is being open to a new experience. That's something I'm always up for. Just name it, and I'll do it, especially when it comes to the arts.

About a decade ago, I dabbled in art. I never officially took a class, but I created some cute drawings using fine markers and colored pencils.

The drawings were okay, but what made them special were my clever plays on words that accompanied them. On blind energy, I made prints of my work and had enough nerve to set up shop in Union Square in New York City, before artists had to have permits to sell on the street. Surprisingly, I sold quite a few. It's not something I ever took as seriously as writing, but nowadays, on occasion, I'll treat myself to an art class. I really love it!

And not long ago, I was thrilled to take singing lessons for several months. It was never my aspiration to sing professionally, but the fact that I can now sing on key around the house is exciting and fun. Who knows— maybe someday I'll try karaoke.

Being open also means being open-minded and creating space in your life for people who will make a positive difference. Opening your heart and mind to new people and new experiences is what enables you to grow, both personally and professionally.

It's so important to learn about different perspectives, cultures, and values, because openness creates empathy and compassion.

A 2014 article published by *Scientific American* reported that research has shown that socially diverse groups are more creative and work harder than homo-geneous groups, which yields better decision making and problem solving. That's because when we work with individuals who are different, we learn to account for new viewpoints and see a bigger picture.

I'm tolerant of perspectives different from mine, but that wasn't always the case. In my thirties, I had some stomach issues and came to the dead-set belief that a raw-food diet was the healthiest way to live and no other way was right. Eating raw foods means consuming only fresh food, nothing from a package or a can or heated on a stove. Raw food is mostly fruits and vegetables but also nuts and seeds. (You can get extremely creative using a dehydrator and come up with incredible delightful dishes.)

I was the thinnest I'd ever been in my life, and I was eating constantly. People were concerned about how skinny I was. When people would question my diet, I'd get defensive. I'd eat in restaurants only if they served raw food, and I limited my friendships by spending time only with people who were raw foodists and vegetarians.

Over time, I decided the raw-food lifestyle wasn't for me. There was no one "Aha!" moment that changed my mind; I just grew and evolved. I still eat healthfully today, but I don't obsess about food and health.

When you get stuck in one hard line of thinking, you hold yourself back. And when you spend time only with people who are just like you, it prevents you from growing. Getting out of your comfort zone enables you to improve yourself and expand your awareness. By going back to healthful cooked foods, I realized two things: You don't have to be a raw foodist to be healthy, and you don't have to be a vegetarian to love animals.

I also learned the dangers of rigid, closed-off thinking. I believe it's vital to stay open-minded and to widen your circle of friends and associates. It's easy for people to get complacent by being the big fish in a small pond. Those people surround themselves with "yes men" who always agree. The big fish can do no wrong, so he or she never has to venture outside the usual comfort zone. And the big fish never grow or improve. They don't challenge themselves.

"Big fish" people remind me of Elvis Presley. Based on accounts of his final years, the man known as the King of Rock 'n' Roll seemed to surround himself with people who would never dare say no to him. As a result, his life of excess led to his death at the age of forty-two in 1977.

When our inner circle includes people who aren't afraid to disagree with us, that can help us make better decisions. Abraham Lincoln was a great president because he put people in his cabinet who thought differently than he did. It's a wise person who seeks out those who can be strong in areas where he or she is weak.

Then there's the simple fact that never doing anything new or meeting anyone different is just plain boring. Without challenges to stimulate your brain, you can become a dullard. Think about when you meet people who look back on high school as the best years of their lives—don't you feel sorry for them? They were comfortable "back in the day," and they never expanded their horizons.

In order to keep growing, you must keep diversity in your social circle. One way to do that is to get involved in a variety of activities. There are so many groups and organizations that bring together different types of people. The possibilities for growth are endless. You can join a gym, take a class, volunteer, or even get a part-time job. You can make a new friend, or at least form a nice new acquaintance, just by asking some basic questions. All it requires is making the first move and being open to the unknown.

In my town in New Jersey, I favor a certain gas station because the owner is so very nice. When I pull into the parking lot, his face lights up. He's happy to see me because I always offer a kind word and some brief conversation. I ask him about his country of origin, India. We talk about holidays, the weather, how our day is going. It all started with a joke that broke the ice and helped us form a connection.

On a similar note, whenever I go to an ethnic restaurant, I try to pronounce the dishes in the native language. And I learn to say thank you in the corresponding language. For example, when I'm in a Japanese restaurant, I'll say, "*Arigato.*" It means so much to people when you make an extra effort to show you appreciate their culture and heritage.

You never know who can make an impact on your life, so don't let age, gender, race, creed, or a belief system stand in the way of making a cool friend!

Looking back at my life, it seems most of my friends have been people with whom I have little in common. When I pointed out to someone that I honestly felt I didn't really fit in anywhere 100 percent because my interests are so varied, that friend said, "That's because you're truly an individual."

If you are open to making friends, you can meet them anywhere and any way, especially when you least expect it—like at the gas station! Those friends might be just like you, nothing like you, or somewhere in between.

When my first book was published, I complained to my husband that some friends and family members weren't being supportive and buying my book. Dennis's response was genius: "You don't want the people who know you and love you to buy your books. You want people you *don't* know to buy them."

That is so true! How else would you develop a fan base if only people you knew purchased your books?

During one of my first book talks, amongst hordes of friends, in walked a large group of young people we didn't know. Dennis nudged me and whispered, "This is exactly what you want."

As I was speaking to the audience, I noticed a young lady who kept making eye contact with me. She seemed to be relating to every word I said.

After the talk, when I was signing books, the young woman, Ashley, approached me right away and said, "You're my future!" It turned out she also wanted to become a writer, and we both had the same favorite band, HIM. We also loved animals and shared the same political beliefs. But there was a huge age gap between us—in fact, I'm Ashley's mom's age!

At my book signing, Ashley was on a date with a guy who ended up becoming her husband. A few months before the wedding, Ashley asked if I'd officiate her wedding. It wasn't something I'd ever done before, but I said I'd do it for her as a wedding gift. In the end, other than my own wedding, this one was my favorite of all time. My husband agreed.

By being open to new people and new things, I was able to have an incredible experience and be part of a young couple's happiest day.

I've also had friends who were a few decades older than I. When I was a young journalist, our entertainment editor, Julie, was in her seventies. She was my favorite person in the office. Julie came to work every day looking like a movie star: in full makeup, with perfectly highlighted hair, and wearing great clothes with matching jewelry. She was incredibly hip and went out every night of the week. Julie never spoke about mundane things like doing laundry, yet when you visited her home, it was immaculate. I always secretly wondered when she had the time to clean, since she was always out and about. I truly admired her.

When it comes to forming friendships, my only requirement is the other person must be willing to be a truly good friend, because I know I will be one. I have friends of all genders, races, creeds, and belief systems. By having so many different types of friends, I am always learning and always enjoying new opportunities.

Sometimes it's amazing how similar people are to you even though you think they're different. When I first joined the group to improve my public speaking, I felt I stood out like a sore thumb. In a room full of people dressed conservatively, there I was with purple hair and shoes that had candy inside the heels! But when I presented a speech on David Bowie, I found out that 80 percent of the members loved David Bowie just as much as I did. Lesson learned: Do not judge a book by the cover.

My public-speaking group includes a great variety of people of all ages and nationalities. That diversity is where the magic comes from. From young to old, regardless of our cultural backgrounds, we all get along and support one another. When someone is so different from you but can appreciate what you bring to the table—and vice versa—it's more than professional. It's kindness and love.

My friend Stephen is a Black man in his late sixties. We've shared stories of being bullied as children and discussed how it's so sad the way politics separates people. One of the coolest things Stephen has said is, "We [human beings] have more things in common than not."

I agree. We all want love. We all want friendships. And we all want to be successful in life. But even in our differences, we can learn from one another. By being open-minded and accepting individuals just as they are, we hear stories that astonish us and our worlds grow so much larger.

In high school, you had your subcultures: goths, punks, jocks, the popular crowd, hip-hop, nerds, stoners, etc. At that age, people name-call or don't want to associate with someone from a different crowd. The thing is, people who continue to live that way are missing out on so much. We're all human beings. We all have issues, but we all have good things about us too. And if you're in school together or you work together, it's highly likely you have at least something in common. You can start a conversation about a particular class or a workplace project. Once you establish that common ground, you can move beyond small talk and see what other interests or beliefs you share.

Think about the odd-couple friendship of Supreme Court justices Antonin Scalia and Ruth Bader Ginsburg. The famously conservative Scalia opposed the court's recognition of gay and lesbian rights. Meanwhile, the liberal-leaning Ginsburg was the first justice to preside over a same-sex marriage. Their views couldn't have been more different. Despite their opposing philosophies, Scalia and Ginsburg established a highly bonded friendship. They shared a love of the law and of opera, made each other laugh, and even traveled to India together.

Can you see yourself hanging out with someone who thinks vastly differently from you? If you give it a try, you might be pleasantly surprised. Otherwise, you might end up leading a very stressful (and lonely) life, arguing with people and proving your points instead of trying to make genuine human connections.

It's easy to meet people who are different from you when you are open and ready for it. Sometimes that means drifting away from people who are no longer serving you. Face it: We all outgrow certain people in our lives, and we must make a conscious effort to move on.

And that's a good thing. Being honest with yourself about knowing when to let go can make an incredible difference. A few years ago, I let go of two friends who seemed to be going in circles in their lives. I tried to be a good friend and give creative suggestions on how to make their lives better. Instead, they chose to continue drinking like fish instead of elevating themselves to a better place. They also chose to stick with the same people, those who encouraged their unhealthy behavior.

If those friends ever decide to change for the better, I'll be there with open arms, welcoming them back into my life. But what I've learned is that when negative people are no longer dragging you down, it opens space for more people to come into your life, bringing light and goodness. Whether these new people are just like you or are a little different, the fact that they are positive and can challenge you is a wonderful thing!

chapter nine

(BE)BRAVE

It's a risk in itself if you don't take risks in life.

Don't you feel sad for people who talk about hating their jobs, yet they stay put? I've heard stories of people staying at the same dead-end job for over thirty years. They feel that leaving would be too risky, too much left to chance. But when you keep doing something that isn't challenging or life-giving, you're taking an even bigger risk—the risk of looking back on your life with deep regret.

There's no reason to feel stuck, because there's always something else around the corner. While you're working on sending out resumes, you can also create a side hustle. Lots of people are generating income doing things they love on the side while they work their day jobs. Or, you can further educate yourself so you have more options down the line.

The thing is, you must take a chance to see what awaits. Nothing ventured, nothing gained. If your boss is uncaring or your career is unsatisfying, or if your co-workers are a bunch of gossips, why stay? Don't you deserve more in life?

On more than one occasion, I've quit a job without having something else lined up. My mind-set was, *I don't know where I'm going, but I'm certainly not staying here!*

In my younger days, I'd find a new job quickly because there wasn't much at stake. But as I get older, I'm more about the ideal situation, because life is short. That's why I work for myself. It's risky being my own boss and having those lulls when business isn't great. But I'm always willing to ride the storm because it's so gratifying when I'm back on top, charging top dollar for my services, making my own hours, and even turning down work if I don't think the client is a good fit. And of course, it goes without saying, I love what I do!

That's how I've learned you must be brave. You can't let your fears control you. Getting out of your comfort zone and saying yes to opportunity will help you grow. When you're brave, something really great can happen. Yes, of course, something negative could happen, too. But do you want to live asking, "What if?" Think about the opportunity cost, the way doing something that doesn't feed you also takes up time when you could be doing something that serves your true self. It's best to take a chance.

Just remember that taking risks does require patience, too. When I first began working for myself, my father-in-law often reminded me, "Rome wasn't built in a day." Your dreams will never come true if you're not patient enough to wait for them to manifest. When successful people appear to be overnight successes, that's almost never the case. It takes a long time to become an overnight success.

The major difference between successful people and ordinary people is that successful people are not afraid to fail. In order to be a success, it's normal to fail many times. In fact, the world is full of successful failures! Did you know Stephen King's most successful book, *Carrie,* was rejected by thirty publishers? Did you know Oprah Winfrey was fired from one of her first jobs because a producer said she was "unfit for television news"? Did you know Thomas Edison's teachers told him he was "too stupid to learn anything"?

Then there are those who were successful but really hit it big later in life. For example, Laura Ingalls Wilder was forty-three when her daughter encouraged her to write her memoir. Vera Wang was an accomplished figure skater and fashion editor when, at age forty, she wanted to become a designer—and the rest is history.

Life is incredible when you have dreams and never give up on them. Even if your dreams are daring or unpopular, you must recognize it's your life you're living. And it's a short one. With no guarantees of how long you'll be around, it's wise to make a conscious effort to fulfill your dreams. Sometimes, even after you've achieved your dreams, you still have to put up a brave fight. As an author of four books, I've received quite a few bad reviews. That didn't stop me from writing. Some of the bad reviews I took as feedback, which helped me become a better writer. Others were written mean-spiritedly. Unfortunately, that can happen when you achieve success. Human nature is that some people simply won't like to see you succeed. But you can't let that stop you. If people don't want to see you succeed, they are not part of your tribe. Just move on.

Better yet, surround yourself with those who are successful. That also takes some bravery.

Years ago, I heard the saying, "If you want to be successful, hang out with four successful people and eventually you will be the fifth." At one time, that thought made me uncomfortable. Imagine hanging out with people who have more money than you, who are happier with their jobs, happier with their lives—intimidating, right? But actually, it's a good thing! Would you rather spend time with people who keep screwing up their lives?

I had a few friends I'd known most of my adult life. They were always dragging me down, but I did everything I could to keep the friendships going because there was so much history. Ultimately, it got to a point where I was becoming more and more frustrated with them because they were like lumps on a log. They never did anything to elevate themselves. Plus, they were never happy when good things—that I worked hard for—happened to me. That's not a friend. So, after much thought, I told those people I wished them no ill will, but the friendship wasn't working out anymore. It takes courage to recognize when you need to part ways with someone and end a bad relationship.

Whatever it is you need to be brave about, the fact that you feel the fear but still choose to act upon it is wonderful. I'm terrified to fly, and it often happens that I'm flying alone for a business trip. It's not just the flying that bothers me, it's the possibility of being stuck for hours in an airport due to delays. I get homesick, and I hate living out of a suitcase. But the thing is, I do it because I don't want to miss out on the opportunities. Being brave doesn't mean being fearless; it's about conquering your fears and moving forward in spite of them.

To conquer your fears, you first need to own them. If you deny your fear, or try to avoid it, it will be detrimental to your success. Facing the fact that you are afraid is the first step to becoming triumphant. You can acknowledge that paranoid inner voice that's your own worst critic and respond to it by saying, "I've got this!"

Remember: Playing it safe is very risky. How will you feel a year from now if you don't make that necessary change in your life? If you're in a bad relationship but fear leaving, a year from now you'll still be in that bad relationship. It's tempting to focus on what could go wrong if you leave your comfort zone, so flip the script and think about what could go right. Picture yourself a year from now: You've left that bad relationship and now you're in a good one with someone incredible. Or, you're discovering your strength and enjoying the freedom of being on your own. That can never happen if you're hanging on to your old baggage.

Every single person has the capability of being happy and successful, and it often starts with being brave. The more you take chances and venture out of your comfort zone, the "luckier" you'll be. Doors will open. You'll meet new people. You'll feel better about yourself in the process. Put it out to the universe that your mind is made up and you're taking your first big step, then go from there.

When you take brave, bold steps, you can inspire others to do the same. I've lost track of how many people have told me I've inspired them to quit their jobs and start their own businesses. Some are more successful than I am. And I love it! How cool is it to have a bunch of warriors in your tribe? People say to themselves: *If she can do it, so can I.* And it's not about competition, it's about encouragement. What feels better than knowing your vision inspired someone else to create their own?

Being brave builds confidence and encourages you to take even more risks. In the beginning, start with small steps. Making one small move toward your goal is better than not moving at all.

Bravery means different things to different people. We all have different fears and different comfort levels. For example, I expressed my fear of flying earlier, but many people embrace flying. Some people don't like to do things alone. But I'm all about doing things on my own. I'll go shopping alone, go to concerts alone, take long drives alone. I'll even do what most people dread: dine alone. Some see that as brave, but it's always been an incredible experience for me. I'll have great talks with waitresses or waiters. People at other tables will strike up conversations with me, or I'll read a few chapters of a book. It's wonderful. If dining alone is something you're afraid to do, I suggest trying it. If you're always saying no, perhaps it's time to say yes.

Conversely, if you're always doing what other people want you to do, speaking up for yourself takes a lot of courage. But in the long run, you're better off putting yourself first. It's your life, so the experiences you want to have should be placed in the forefront. Be brave in risking what your friends—or even family—might think.

Speaking up for yourself and for others in the face of opposition is truly heroic. You might do that by donating your time and money to political or social causes that matter to you. Or, you might do it on an individual level, speaking one-on-one with someone about an issue that's close to your heart.

For example, I get very upset when I hear gossip. To me, it's a form of bullying, and whenever I hear someone gossiping—whether it's about me or about someone else—you can bet I will say something to stop it. I believe everyone should.

Some time ago, I was told by an acquaintance that her friend was gossiping about me. My mouth dropped open and I was speechless. I was disappointed, not only at the one who was talking trash but at the acquaintance who apparently had done or said nothing to put an end to it. So, I spoke up.

"Did you tell your friend that it's unbecoming to talk bad about others?" I asked.

"No. She talks bad about everyone," she replied.

"Did you ask your friend if it makes her feel better about herself if she talks bad about others?"

"No."

Finally, I said, "And why are *you* friends with this person who is so negative?"

She told me she felt sorry for her.

With that, I turned on my heels and walked away. I didn't want to hear anymore, and I felt I'd made my point. I was proud to have put my two cents in and to have made it clear that gossip is unacceptable to me.

Taking a stand is something to feel good about. It takes some practice, but if you don't advocate for yourself and for the things you feel strongly about, who will? Yes, sometimes people will argue with you or take offense at your beliefs. But you never know. You could be just the person who can inspire someone else to make a change. That person might not tell you, but the fact that you planted a seed is something to be proud of.

So, make a mental note that you'll speak up the next

time you hear or see something you know isn't right. You might not change the world, but changing your inner circle is something honorable and worthwhile.

Also, take some time to think about all the things you would do or say if you weren't afraid. Make a list. Then, one by one, make a plan to try to do all (or at least some of) the things on that list.

Any positive change, any time you say your piece, any time you do something daring—it's a great accomplishment. You are making a difference, and that is truly heroic!

chapter ten

(BE)BALANCED

In today's face-paced world, many of us are saying yes to things we aren't truly connecting with.

We say yes because we want people to like us. We say yes because we want to be part of a group. We say yes because we want to be a hero.

Saying yes sometimes is good. It's great to be giving and to do things for others. But it's not so good when saying yes puts us in a place that's uncomfortable, unhealthy, or unbalanced.

Not too long ago, I worked for a small media company. I loved the job, but there was no work/life balance. I felt like I was a character in *The Devil Wears Prada* trying to keep up with a grueling schedule and endless demands. Saying yes and burning myself out wasn't worth the pay or the professional experience. So, I quit. My mental, emotional, and physical health were more important.

Don't get me wrong—I'm no stranger to hard work, especially since I love what I'm doing. But we live in a time when people see "busy" as a status symbol and fail to see the negatives of sleep deprivation and chronic stress. Without down time to do fun things with those you love, even if it's just a Sunday off, you can't possibly sustain a successful career.

The bottom line is, we're human beings, not machines. And it's our prerogative to say no when we're running out of gas and/or feeling unappreciated. It's necessary to create boundaries. We must realize our needs are just as important as everyone else's, even in a place of business. If you feel you're being taken advantage of, you probably are.

Happiness is a choice. So, it's vital to move past your fear and learn how to speak up for yourself. It's also key to remember that if something isn't satisfying to you, whether it's your job or a relationship, you can choose to let it go. That can be scary! But if your gut is saying no to something, you should listen. "Go with your gut" became a cliché because it's truly great advice.

Saying no isn't always easy. It takes practice to be assertive regarding what *you* want. But in the long run, putting yourself first is the best thing you can do not only for yourself but for your loved ones. Remember, everyone is in different places in their lives. It's okay to want to connect with those who are on the same page you are. If you have good seats to see a band you've always wanted to see but then a destination-wedding invitation shows up in your mailbox, it's okay to decline. And you don't owe anyone an explanation for doing what is right for you.

One of my best friends declines in a most eloquent

manner. She begins by saying, "I can't make it," then offers a different plan on a future date. Compromise and negotiation can be awesome alternatives to saying yes when you don't really want to.

Saying no to things that don't suit you is, at its core, about letting go of feeling guilty. It's about saying, "It's time for me!" It's about making choices and putting your needs first.

While promoting her bestselling memoir, *Becoming*, Michelle Obama opened up about the reality of trying to have it all. As she put it, you *can* have it all—just not all at the same time. After decades of balancing a high-powered career, parenting, and public life, the former first lady learned the hard way that you simply can't excel at—and say yes to—everything all at once. When you try to do that, the best-case scenario is being mediocre at things you care about. The worst-case scenarios include disappointment, resentment, broken dreams, and a feeling of defeat.

Deciding to accept our limits and set boundaries is positively countercultural. Social media is, at least in part, responsible for creating the phenomenon of FOMO: fear of missing out. If we're doing one thing, we're thinking about or wishing we were doing something else. We're forgetting to appreciate what we *do* have, what we *are* doing, and who we *are* with. There's always something else we need to be chasing, right? Something else to have, do, gain, win, or accomplish.

Ironically, by saying yes to that pressure, we're very often saying no to our real dreams—to the people, places, and things that make us genuinely happy.

One of my favorite success stories is that of Sonny and Cher. As aspiring stars, they were once so down on their luck, their furniture was repossessed. It was then that Sonny Bono wrote one of the duo's greatest hits: "I Got You Babe." He didn't have much else, but he had the woman he loved, and she had him. And that sincere expression of love is a song that has endured for generations—even though their marriage ultimately didn't—making Sonny and Cher icons in the process.

So, as you work on being direct and clear with others, don't forget to be direct and clear with yourself. Understand what really matters to you. Develop a structure to achieve your goals. Make conscious decisions about what you need to do in order to succeed. Be mindful of who you spend your time with, and make sure those people believe in you and your goals.

When you say no often enough to things that don't serve you, you'll see there's so much time to do things that *do* serve you. Suddenly there's time for the gym! Now there's time for a painting class! Now there's time to redecorate your home! How did all that happen? You asserted yourself and made yourself a priority in your own life. It was that easy.

So, do you "have it all"? It depends on what you feel is "having it all." Again, this is *your* life you're living. Don't define your blueprint by someone else's.

A few years ago, there was a story circulating around Facebook. Whether it's true or not is irrelevant; it's the message that was inspiring. The story was about a bond fund CEO who earned more than a hundred million dollars a year. But the man resigned unexpectedly to spend more time with his ten-year-old daughter. It all happened after they had a fight. She didn't do something he told her to do, and he yelled at her, "I'm your father and you will do what I say!" She then went to her room and created a list of twenty-two important moments in her life, such as birthday parties and school events, that her father had missed because of his career.

That story illustrates that no matter how much you do, something else in your life will suffer. It's all a matter of perspective. Some people want to work for six-pack abs; they enjoy time in the gym and the sense of accomplishment they get from looking great. Other people don't mind having a little extra gut because they'd prefer to be home in the evenings to walk their dogs, devour a new novel, or get some extra sleep. It's not right or wrong—it's just making the choices that are best for *you*.

The thing is, there are so many opportunities to do things for ourselves, to do things for others, and to do things for our careers. We live in a wonderful time when there are many options available to us. It's entirely up to us where we want to put our energies and where we want to sacrifice. It can actually be a bit overwhelming!

The beauty is knowing that our "having it all" doesn't have to match someone else's.

Perhaps the best approach is to change our mind-set from "having it all" to "having a sweet balance." Celebrate your life for where you are right now. Don't become so busy that you have no time to enjoy the everyday pleasures. It's impossible to change overnight, but if you keep reminding yourself how important "me time" is, you'll fall into an awesome pattern of putting yourself first. Everything else will flow from there.

Also remember that almost nothing is set in stone. If you say no to something, you usually can change your mind to yes if you're feeling up to it later. And vice versa: If you said yes, you can change your mind to no. Try not to worry about disappointing someone else. It's more important—and more valuable—to be honest with yourself. You'll know when you're on the right track to something good.

As with anything else in life, becoming direct and assertive takes time and effort. It's said that it takes about twenty days to develop a good habit. You can keep track of your good habits by journaling. Write down the times when you communicated clearly what you wanted or didn't want. Note the exact language you used and how you felt being direct. After about three weeks, look back and see the progress you've made. How many times did you say no? Did it get easier as time went on? When you said no to something you didn't want to do, did you instead use that time to do something you really wanted to do?

Time spent on yourself is always time well-spent, even if it's just fifteen minutes per day to meditate, take a walk, do something artistic, etc. A friend of mine once shared that she likes to sit alone with her cup of coffee in the morning. Her family knows not to bother her during that time. Personally, I like to decompress by playing games on the computer for a half-hour midday. I turn off my email and Facebook alerts just so I can have that time to unwind. Then, I can go back to the real world.

Nothing feels better than having some extra time for yourself. You can have the best co-workers, the best spouse, and the best family; it's still important to make yourself a priority. You might even build up the amount of time you set aside once you see how good it feels.

If you're having a hard time finding balance in your life, you might not be fully aware of what's important to you. Or, you might feel a bit sheepish about being honest about what you'd like to prioritize. Imagine if you had a day off to do whatever you wanted. What would you place on top of the list? Don't feel like you're a bad relative or a bad friend if your ideal list is more focused on you than on others. It might be a sign that you're currently feeling depleted by the many demands in your life, and you need to get back in touch with your own wants and needs.

On weekends when I was a kid, my mom used to say, "I can't wait to get back to the office—that's where I get peace." My mom certainly loved her family. But she needed the time at work to focus on other things and make herself a whole person.

Ask yourself if you're being consistent about meeting your own needs. If you'd decided you wanted more time for yourself, but then slowly started caving to the needs of others, then allow yourself to start over and change your pattern. Don't give up! Be direct and assertive about what you need—both from yourself and from others. Don't allow *you* to treat yourself as an afterthought.

When you realign your life to that sweet balance, you will feel happier, more energetic, and more in control of your life and your future.

Congratulations—you've become your own hero!

(BE)ACTIVE

Make a list of five people you consider heroes. What traits do you admire about them? Which of those characteristics do you want or need to work on in your life?

_____

_____

_____

_____

_____

_____

_____

_____

_____

_____

_____

_____

_____

_____

_____

_____

_____

_____

_____

_____

_____

To practice the tip from chapter one, write down your achievements up to today. Then, identify at least one thing you want to accomplish tomorrow. Look back one year from now and see how far you've come!

_____

_____

_____

_____

_____

_____

_____

_____

_____

_____

_____

_____

_____

_____

_____

_____

_____

_____

_____

_____

_____

_____

_____

Practice journaling about gratitude and giving as I suggest in chapter six. Make a list of five things for which you're grateful today. Then, make a list of five kind things you've done for others recently. Take a few moments to reflect on how you felt after each of those experiences.

_____

_____

_____

_____

_____

_____

_____

_____

_____

_____

_____

_____

_____

_____

_____

_____

_____

_____

_____

_____

_____

_____

_____

_____

Write about a time when you were direct and clear about something important to you. How did you feel when you were assertive? Then, recall a time when you struggled to advocate for yourself. How did you feel, and how did the situation turn out?

_____

_____

_____

_____

_____

_____

_____

_____

_____

_____

_____

_____

_____

_____

_____

_____

_____

_____

_____

_____

_____

_____

What are some things you've done in your life that someone might see as heroic?

_____

_____

_____

_____

_____

_____

_____

_____

_____

_____

_____

_____

_____

_____

_____

_____

_____

_____

_____

_____

_____

_____

_____

_____

_____

_____

List ten things you love and embrace about yourself.

_____

_____

_____

_____

_____

_____

_____

_____

_____

_____

_____

_____

_____

_____

_____

_____

_____

_____

_____

_____

_____

_____

_____

_____

_____

_____

(BE)INTENTIONAL

Space for Reflection and Planning

_____

_____

_____

_____

_____

_____

_____

_____

_____

_____

_____

_____

_____

_____

_____

_____

_____

_____

_____

_____

_____

_____

_____

_____

_____

_____

_____

_____

_____

_____

_____

_____

_____

_____

_____

_____

_____

_____

_____

_____

_____

_____

_____

_____

_____

_____

_____

_____

_____

_____

_____

_____

_____

_____

_____

_____

BE (EXTRA)ORDINARY

BE (EXTRA)ORDINARY

BE (EXTRA)ORDINARY

ACKNOWLEDGMENTS

To my husband, Dennis Mistretta, for always believing in me. I love you with all my heart and soul. I'm beyond blessed to be your wife.

To Grandma, in heaven. If it wasn't for you, I wouldn't be the person I am today. You taught me to live life to the fullest and to "take a chance." I'm forever grateful.

To Pop Mistretta, in heaven, for showing me the ropes with business and always reminding me, "Rome wasn't built in a day."

To my brother-in-law Joe. Thanks so much for your love and support.

To Mommy. You taught me some amazing things, but the best thing you ever said to me when I was a little girl was: "Don't be jealous of anyone. If someone has something you want, be happy for them."

To Jayne DiGregorio, the "Michele" to my "Romy." It's always a great idea to hang out with people who bring out the best in you. Jayne, you have gone above and beyond this. You're always the first to call and make a plan—for business or just for fun. And you're there when I need a friend to talk to. I love our adventures and look forward to more! Keep rockin' it, girlfriend. Here's to our Business Woman's Lunches and much more! I love you! (And thanks to Jayne's super-cool life partner, Rob, for being a great friend too!)

To Joan Brusco-Bunda, Darlene Foster, Shaolin, and Kimberly Redl. Thanks so much for being a part of my High Five Tribe! I'm so happy, and honored, to have all of you in my life.

To bestselling author and radio/television personality Maryann Castello, for having me twice on your Health & Wellness show to promote my books! Maryann, you are such a doll, gorgeous inside and out, with the most amazing aura. Thank you!

To Rebecca Benston, publisher of Higher Ground Books. You are one of my biggest Facebook supporters for this book! You are such a beautiful, kind, and thoughtful person, and I appreciate you.

To Oleda Baker, Scott Schiaffo, and Robyn Lane. Thanks so much for your generous endorsements. I admire and look up to each of you so much. It was an honor for you to write such great things about this book. Wow—just wow!

To our beautiful kitty, Nicholas Gray. You simply make life wonderful with your playful antics. Just keep working the cute. Mommy and Daddy love you!

To our newest addition to the family, our sweet, big-eyed kitty, Sammy Keane Clemens.

And to our little kitty hearts waiting for us on the Rainbow Bridge: Billy Cat Mistretta, Derick Lords, and of course, Bennie Grover Hemingway. You've all left paw prints on our hearts, you little rascals!

Printed in the United States
By Bookmasters